I Remember Warm Rain

15 Teenagers
15 coming to America Stories

The Telling Room's Story House Project
Photographs by Laura Lewis

I Remember
Warm Rain

15 Teenagers
15 coming to America Stories

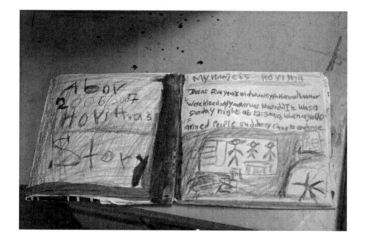

Ali Mohamed's Storybook

Introduction:
Shelter

A girl is telling her story, about the doves her father once kept in Afghanistan. The words lift as they leave her mouth. They carom in the corners of the room, spin, and zoom back. Her father was a good man who one day found himself on the way to the vegetable market when he got caught in a crossfire. His third of five daughters is remembering him now: the cooing sound of his voice as he spoke to his birds, how he painted the tops of their heads pink and yellow to make them pretty, how they always flew back to him. Remembering those birds makes her smile. After what happened to her father, she started a journey to America that took years, to this place called Portland, Maine.

The girl is a junior at Deering High School. Her name is Aqila Sharafyar—and she is one of the fifteen students, from countries such as Somalia, Iraq, Sudan, and Iran, represented in this anthology. Soon you will meet Ali killing hyenas and Aruna speaking to his father by phone after ten years of believing he is dead. You will meet Kahiye, reveling in his first experience of snow, and Stella doing something once forbidden to her, playing a game she loves: soccer.

As stories are told, they develop their own structure. They grow walls and extra rooms and windows through which one spies new landscapes of color, sound, and memory, the birds flying in blue ether, the spaces between sentences filling with silence. Or laughter. Or a single gasp.

These are stories—real stories belonging to real American teenagers—that deserve not just our attention but shelter as well: a safe place between these covers where they may find a sort of permanence, as acts of historical remembrance, and where we can visit them again and again.

This has been the abiding idea and animating force behind The Telling Room's Story House Project, a multi-media project built on the collaborative efforts of local artists, writers, filmmakers, sound technicians, teachers, and the 15 young storytellers here who have bravely told their tales of leaving home in hopes of finding a new one in America.

What is the Story House Project? It is an attempt to make these stories three dimensional by housing them inside of actual structures, to give them a sensual reality, in images, sound, and text, that leaves an indelible mark. It is governed by an idea that we can move in and out of one another's lives—one another's figurative story houses—truly listening for, and hopefully finding one another.

What follows in these pages is the actual foundation of this project, the 15 amazing stories on which everything else has been built, some labored over for more than a year. For some of the students here, the triumph has been to make sentences in a language that's new to them; for others, it has been to put across the big ideas of their lives, with emotion and humor.

We at The Telling Room hope that the inner life of our community becomes that much deeper when we share stories such as these. What more is there to say? Without the commitment and hard work of young storytellers like Aqila, Abdiaziz, Ali, Aruna, Estella, Farah, Hamid, Hashim, Hassan, Jackson, Kahiye, Mohamed Rashid, Nasra, Navid, and Ridwan, we'd have nothing but a bunch of blank pages. So we are pleased and proud to have you read the stories that follow. Having spent a lot of time in their company, we promise they'll move you, too.

Stories

Aruna Kenyi reading his story

The Photograph

Aruna Kenyi

I am seventeen years old and I have no photographs of my past—none of my village or parents or me as a boy there, none of the places where we fled or the camps in which we lived, nor of my friends.

For instance, I've never seen a picture of my oldest brother, and I will never know what he looked like. He was a captain in the army, and he was killed the year I was born, 1989. So that's why my parents gave me his name.

Kenyi.

I was born in the village of Nyepo, in southern Sudan. I was one of the youngest of nine brothers and sisters. We grew corn, and had chickens and goats. There were banana groves nearby and a river that ran very deep during the rainy season. I drank from that river every day, and every other person born in my village drank from it, too.

My father was a farmer. He had a very calm voice. That's what I remember. He never went to school, just grew the food to help his family survive. He was also a soldier, and once after he accidentally dropped his rifle in the water, they put him in prison.

I'm told that I'm tall like him, but look more like my mother. She had lots of hair—and was really fast. If I did something wrong and tried to run away, she always caught me.

My village was happiness. That's what I remember. And Christmas was the best day of the year. All the families played together, to all hours of the night. We ate bananas and played drums. We made guns out of branches and acted like we were soldiers, too. We hid and captured each other in the banana grove. Some of us pretended we were children and some pretended we were parents.

I will tell you now about the night everything changed. It was the hour just after dinner when families go to visit each other. Everybody gets up and wanders from place to place, saying their hellos. My tribe, the Bari—we're very friendly people. I was with three of my brothers, playing. I would have been five years old. Meanwhile, my parents had gone to our garden, to pick corn.

That's when the Arab militia attacked. Everything was peaceful, and then I heard a noise like an earthquake. I saw the plane coming, and they started bombing our village. Then they came in trucks. The soldiers were yelling at us to leave our homes, and they started killing people and burning everything.

Of course, everyone ran in a different direction to save his or her life. Some mothers and fathers even forgot their kids. That's how I was separated from my parents. My brother led us into a cane field and we hid there for the night. We could see the fires and hear the screaming. There were many mosquitoes and the grass was sharp and wet on my face.

In the morning there was nothing left. No houses, nothing. My oldest brother, who was 20 at the time, said, "It's no use. Our parents are probably dead, and we don't want to die here, too," so we got up from the field and started walking. "I'd rather die ahead," he said.

I just wanted my parents, that's all I remember. From that point on my life has been one of never getting to say goodbye.

So we walked for a year, through different tribes' lands: the Koko, the Mari. Some were friendly; some were not. It was very far for a young boy, and my brothers sometimes carried me. We ended up in a camp in Uganda called Kali. There were many lost children—and a lot of disease and death. It was there that we met my uncle and where he was shot and stoned when Ugandan rebels attacked. They burned houses with people in them, like before, and we ran again and hid in the fields by the mountains.

During this time I thought about my mother and father. I could remember them taking care of us. We would have a bath every night. I was a really bad kid, so they were always having to punish me. When I was hungry, my mother would say, "If you don't want to work, then there's no food for you today." These were the lessons I learned.

Sometimes my brothers would tell stories about them and when they did, it made me believe that my parents were not dead, like they were here again with us.

Later, we ended up in the camp at Kyangwali. We stayed there five years. I remember it was next to a forest and the monkeys and baboons scared me. I didn't have time for homework. I worked our little garden all the time to try and get food—corn, beans, and nuts. Like my father once had.

And then one day they told us to get ready, that we were going to America. We'd spent years hoping for this moment, and then when it came, we had no time to say goodbye to anyone, none of our good friends, no one. They just put us on a truck and took us to the airport. We left many people there. We flew from Kampala to Nairobi to the UK to New York to Virginia, where we lived for the first year. Then we came to Portland.

We were lucky, my brothers and I. We survived all those years without illness or real harm. We grew up without parents, which was very hard. Every night, in those camps, we'd have to wait two or three hours in line for water because the big people just kept pushing past us. There was no one to protect us.

Not long after coming to Portland we had a letter in the mail, and in that letter, was… a photograph! I don't know how to say this, but it was of my mother and father. They were alive. My mother was standing and my father was sitting in a wheelchair because the soldiers shot his legs off. They looked so old—my father's hair was gray—but I remember looking at that photograph for a very long time. I've since talked to my father on the phone in Sudan. His voice is like I remember it: calm. But he has had a hard life. He said he would like to go back to our village some day, but right now I won't let him.

All of our happiness was there—and it's still not possible to return.

A Day in Three Worlds

Hassan Jeylani

I wake to the sound of my dad's alarm clock—it's loud, insistent, like a fire alarm. I'm in bed, wrapped up in two or three blankets, and through the doorway, I see my dad shaking his head while he tries to loop his tie. I sit up. My clock reads 7:11 a.m. I rub my eyes—am I dreaming, or is my dad actually there, getting ready? He walks over towards me, still adjusting his tie.

"Get up, it's Sunday," he says.

"Huh?"

"It's Sunday, Hassan, get up."

I'm still asleep, but the thought of my dad dressing up on a Sunday morning and telling me to get up puzzles me. I pull my blankets back over my head and pretend this never happened.

He comes back again. He goes to my brother's bed this time, knowing it'll take more than words to get him up. My dad hits my brother's shoulders several times, and Kahiye jumps to his feet.

"I'm awake, I'm awake…The bus doesn't leave for 20 minutes. I've got time," my brother says, still asleep.

My dad laughs, "Waryaatha, it's Ede, get ready, prayers are about to start."

* * *

I had forgotten Ede, the most joyful Muslim holiday. For 15 years I've been celebrating Ede, anticipating it each year. But this year, I didn't wake up with that same excitement. I didn't even know it was Ede until my dad told me. How could I have forgotten?

For most Muslims, Ede is one of the most important days of the year. It comes a couple weeks after Ramadaan, which is 30 days of fasting and is one of the five pillars a Muslim must follow in his lifetime. At 15, Muslim boys and girls are expected to fast for Ramadaan—the fasting allows Muslims to get out of their ordinary lives and put themselves in someone else's shoes. At 15, Muslim boys and girls are supposed to have sworn that there's only one God. At 15, we're supposed to do the five daily prayers. At 15, if possible, we're supposed to give back to the poor. At 15, we're supposed to be dreaming about going on the Hajj once in our lives.

At 15, I barely complete the days of Ramadaan. At 15, I struggle to do the five daily prayers. At 15, I don't have a job or any money to give back to anyone.

* * *

"Allaahu Akbar, Allaahu Akbar, Allaahu Akbar."

I am in the third row, sitting with my legs crossed, my arms on my thighs, repeating the ritual words of the Imam. I am wearing cimmamad and qamiis and a hat, the traditional Muslim clothes. We're in the gym at Portland High School, and everyone has brought their own prayer mats. There are sixty or seventy of us praying with the Imam, less people than last year. The men pray at the front, and where normally there would be a curtain or a wall, instead there's just a space, and the women pray in back of it. As prayers are about to start, a few little boys are running around near where their mothers are about to take stand and pray. I laugh—when I was their age, I was well-dressed and stood next to my dad and prayed with everyone else. When I was their age, I prayed five times a day.

Prayers are optional right now. Not because I've lost faith, but because of the society I live in. Also, I forget it's less than 2 minutes. My mind is set up to go to school, come home, go to sleep.

* * *

In Somalia, where I was born and lived for the first two years of my life, we would wake up in the morning and go to morning prayers on Ede. The stores, the businesses, the meat market, even the guy who walked around with a large covered plate selling sweet candy, took a day off—everything was shut down for the entire day. Morning prayers would be at the mosque; everyone would be there dressed in their traditional clothes.

The inside of the mosque is beautiful, the ceiling decorated with gold and other bright colors, the windows open. I think about a thousand people can fit in there. It's huge. All these people crammed together sitting on the massive rug covering the floor with the Koran in their laps.

There's an Imam at the front. The prayer takes a few minutes, depending on the Imam. Nowadays, little kids would be with their moms, but I remember being with my dad. The women aren't in the back in Somalia, they're completely separate, in a separate room.

After the prayer, you look to the left and to the right and say something that's almost like "Merry Christmas." Then the kids would walk around and get money from everyone. After that, I'd go back to my home, and then I'd be free to do whatever I want. There's no school that day or the next day. I'd try to get out of my traditional clothes.

I'd go outside, walk around. Everyone's out, doing their own thing, sitting under apple and banana trees for the shade. Some kids are playing soccer in the sand.

My dad has changed out of his work clothes, he's wearing the Somalian version of a sarong, sitting on a low stool with jugs of water all around him. It's sort of like you're in the mall, but everyone knows each other and would say--no matter if you're rich, poor, crippled--that Allah was there, God was there, and you're worshiping Him.

* * *

During the war in Somalia, when I was two, my family had flown to Kenya to get away from the chaos. My parents hoped to return, but they knew there was a slim chance of going back.

In Nairobi, there weren't very many Muslims around. As a kid, I'd think, "I'm gonna go pray, if I want, go to school, then maybe go play a little soccer." Ede was still there, but it wasn't the same. Nairobi was so huge, and we lived in the city. The people there were all different. I wasn't used to these huge buildings, and it was very busy.

I remember one time in Nairobi when a girl my older brother's age, Marion, burst through the gate where my brother and I were playing soccer, saying "Let's play." We'd just finished playing one-touch pass, so they got some other older kids to play with them. At three, I knew I was too little to play a pick-up game. Just before the game got started, Marion said, "I need someone to watch out for my dad." Being a Muslim girl, Marion wasn't allowed to play with guys.

Kahiye told me to be the lookout. I climbed up on the tall iron fence and stood sideways on a little ledge watching both the game and for Marion's father. I could see over the fence, my head just above the fence's sharp points. I watched as Marion put the ball between Kahiye's legs and then ran around him and scored. As I watched Marion dancing around the goal, I saw out of the corner of my eye Marion's father walking to the gate. In the excitement of the goal and the fear that Marion would never being able to play again, with my hands gripping the fence points, I tried to jump down, and one of the points sliced my neck.

I fell flat on my back. I saw the birds overhead in the clear, hot sky, my head spinning. My brother picked me up and held me up to his chest and, when he let me back down, blood, my blood covered his shirt.

* * *

Memories like these run through my mind as I walk over to the Y here in Portland to play basketball with my friends, brother, and cousins. This has been my home now for eight years. I change into my basketball shorts and my Jermaine O'Neal high-tops and one of my practice jerseys. My cousins are shooting for teams as I come back from the bathroom. As soon as I see them, I drop to the ground laughing.

"Yo, quit playing around, get changed," I say.

"We're ready man, c'mon," Mustaf says.

Mustaf's got jeans, a black tank-top, and dress-up shoes on. Omar's wearing a white button-down shirt, khaki shorts, and sandals.

"Alright, forget it, let's just play," I say.

What I don't say is that I remember when I was like that, not knowing what to wear, not being used to having so many different kinds of clothes to choose from.

We're playing four on four, full court. Shots are falling for everyone. We're sort of like the "And1" team: it's all about streetball, crossing someone up, throwing no-look passes, talking mad trash. I'm at center court, holding the ball, then Omar's covering me. I look down and laugh at his sandals. I shake him to the right, he doesn't react. I shake him to the left, he still doesn't react. I take off to the right full speed and I can hear his sandals chasing after me. I cross the ball back over to my left hand and for a second I don't hear the flapping of his sandals. Then I hear him drop flat on his ass.

The game stops. I stop. I drop the ball and start laughing. Everyone hovers over him, booing and laughing at how badly he's been faked.

* * *

Kahiye and I are back at home, collapsed on the couches, playing FIFA 2006 on PlayStation 2, still laughing about Omar and his sandals. After a few games, Kahiye gets tired of losing and turns off the system and goes to the fix something to eat. I flip through the channels and put on ESPN. During Sportscenter, there's a commercial for the latest DVD collection of Baywatch. Pamela Anderson running down the beach in her signature red swimsuit.

It was in Nairobi when I started watching American movies, and Baywatch. In Somalia, we didn't have a TV in the house where we lived. We couldn't believe it. Money, cars, houses, all this stuff, Pamela Anderson running by in a bikini. TV gave us our ideas about America. We thought in the US, everything would be handed to you, like gold. You'd get your own house, your own car, a pool.

I remember sitting in my bunk bed in Nairobi, cramped in a small room with my family. It was so hot that we kept checking the fan to see if it was on. It was always on. A commercial would lure us in, showing a fancy house with a pool. Our fantasies would take over. We're living in a mansion in America, my sisters are in the pool while my brother and I are in the house being served by Jeffrey, the butler from the "Fresh Prince of Bel-Air." "Dinner is served, Master Hassan," he would say.

The commercial ends. Kahiye is banging the fan.

* * *

Later, I decide to pray Isha, the last prayer of the day. It takes a couple minutes to do the ritual movements, most of which involve standing, bowing, kneeling, and placing my head on the floor. I used to do it almost every day, but most nights now I run out of time.

After I'm done, I sit on my bed, hands held up high, reciting parts of the Koran. I lie on my back looking at the ceiling and let my mind wander. This is when all the doubts and questions I have start to unfold.

I prayed five times a day in Somalia. In Nairobi, three times. Now, it's none. It's not consistent. The religion is still here, people are here. Prayers and traditions are still here. But Ede's not a holiday, or at least it doesn't feel like it.

Most of the changes have happened because of where we are. If I was in Somalia, things would be less complicated: get up, pray, eat, go to Muslim school, come home, eat, go back to prayer. There, every day revolves around the same quotidian existence. In Somalia, prayer was most important.

I do stop once in a while and think about it. I don't want to forget a single homework assignment. I don't want to forget a single prayer. I don't want to forget a single basketball practice. There's consequences to all three. But there's not enough time to do all three. I even ask for help from religious leaders. "I can't handle school, I can't handle basketball, I can't handle my religion all at once," I say. "How I should balance all of them?" The same answer always comes back: the Koran. In other words, they want me to seek answers myself.

My dad wanted to get us away from the tribal fighting in Somalia. I've started my whole life over. I've gone from having to share a room to having my own. I've gone from having no TV to two TVs and a computer and an iPod. I've gone from barefoot to nine different kinds of shoes.

I've gone from three outfits to a closet full of them.

I appreciate all these precious things and the opportunities I've been given, but there's still an empty hole in my life. I've gained all these things, but I've lost something and I want to recover it. Most nights I fall asleep thinking about all this, but then, two days later, I'm playing basketball at the Y and thinking about Omar and Mustaf, and that thought is gone.

Nasra Hassan

Lost & Found

Nasra Hassan

I remember now
a second ago
I forgot yesterday
the day before
the week before
the month before
the year before.
I forgot.
I wish I could remember
but I forgot.
Now I wish to remember.

I remember the big house in Somalia,
the vegetable garden in the back.
I remember the quiet during the day
when I was home alone with the babysitter.

I forget where everyone was.
I think I remember birds and monkeys in the trees.
I remember stories about monkeys,
but forget the details, forget if I was there.
I remember living surrounded by families;
My father's sisters, my mother's family.
I remember leaving Somalia when I was three.
I don't remember why. I don't remember
any war or anything scary.
I remember the packing of suitcases.
I forget which clothes we put in them.
I remember my brother throwing up in the airplane.
And then him throwing up again on the car ride
away from the airport.
I remember seeing homeless people from this car
window: They were searching the dumps.
I remember being afraid.
I had never seen people so poor.
I remember sleeping squished among
cousins and siblings in one room.
I remember the outdoor feasts during Ramadan

in Mombasa. I remember delicious samosas.
I forget what the houses we stayed in looked like.
I forget what we ate in the mornings.
I remember studying the Koran in Nairobi.
I remember my sister teaching me.
I remember when my father and brother
left for the Unites States in 1997.
I forget what the day was like.
I forget what we said.
I remember when my other brother followed
a couple of months later. I remember the two years
that my mother and I were in Kenya without them.
But I forget what we did, how we lived.
I do remember playing that game with stones.
I remember jumping hopscotch
with kids in the neighborhood.
I forget their faces, their names.
I forget what it was like to be with my mom alone.
I remember how sad I felt on the way to the airport
then in the airplane, feeling better,
looking forward to seeing my family again.

I Remember Warm Rain

I remember my Dad picking me up in Virginia.
I forget how he looked, or what I was wearing.
I forget if anyone else was there.
I forget what we talked about on the long car ride to
   Maine.
I remember my mother staying behind,
staying with her family there in Virginia.
I forget what had happened.
When we got to Maine,
I remember that there was warm rain
at the end of snow season, melting the snow.

I forget the sounds and colors and smells
of my memories, I forget the details, the moments.
I forget day-to-day life.
I remember now.
I remember my house —
forgot the one before it.
I remember the outfit I wore today —
forgot the one I was wearing yesterday.
I remember what I ate today —

forgot what I ate the day before.
I remember my friends now —
forgot the old friends.
I remember what my friends are into now.
I forgot and wonder what the old ones are into now.
I forgot. I forgot, I forgot.

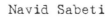

Navid Sabeti

Promises

Navid Sabeti

In grades one through five, in elementary school in a
small village in Iran, I did well. Then, when we moved
to the city, school got harder. In Iran, they have two or
three books about Iran and Islam that you have to learn,
including the Koran. My religion, Bahá'i, says it's not bad
to learn about Islam, so I memorized the Koran like the
other students, but I didn't pray with them or go to the
parades after school. I didn't do well—my grades were
hurt because I wouldn't pray with them.

I would go to my Bahá'ian class on Friday mornings
and learn about my religion and other religions, so then
on Saturdays I would go back to my Koran class and ask
a lot of questions about Islam and the Koran. I would ask
questions like, "Why do the Muslims think the Bahá'ians
are bad?", and the teacher would get angry and tell
me after class not to ask any more questions. He tried

to get me out of the class. The first year I asked a lot of questions, but the next year I was quiet because I didn't want to make any trouble.

My mother said to my father, "Look at the other Bahá'ians who moved to the U.S. Their children are going to be doctors. They're doing really well." My father said, "I was born here. I grew up here. I've been working for twenty years, and I have a car. I'm fine here." It was an old car but it worked. We had plenty of clothes and enough to eat. My father worked so hard. He did admit we had a problem—when we went outside, the Muslims watched us and saw us as different. Also, he knew that I would have to work hard for twenty years just to get what he had.

My father was a farmer in Iran, and he brought vegetables and fruit to the market to be sold. He tried one year to sell the vegetables and fruit himself, but no one wanted to buy them. In Iran, I would have had to be a farmer like my dad, or, if I didn't like it, maybe I could move to another city where no one knows me and drive a taxi. Things like that are all Bahá'ians can do over there.

My father was scared to move. My mother had more courage. My mother said, "Let's go to Turkey so we can move to another country." They didn't know if they wanted to go to Canada or the U.S. or somewhere else. Ten or fifteen years ago, Iranians who wanted to move would go to Pakistan, but now they go to Turkey.

My father was nervous, because we didn't have much money. My mother kept hearing about all the people who left Iran and were doing well, and my father was also tired from working so much. He agreed to move after we saved a little bit of money, but he was still nervous.

When I was thirteen, my parents asked me to make a promise about leaving Iran. My father said, "I have something here. I have a car. I can farm. I can live here, but I don't want you to be like me, and that's why we're moving. You have to make me a promise to work hard and to become something better than me."

I said okay. We sold everything we had and moved to Turkey. I didn't know what was coming; I knew I would miss my friends in Iran. I had made a lot of friends in middle school, and then after two years, we had to move. It was hard to leave all of them. Almost all my friends were Bahá'í—I tried to get along with the Muslim students, but I wasn't friends with them.

I told my friends I was moving to Canada. They said, "You're going to go drink Pepsi over there!" That was a joke we used to make about Canada. We laughed about it. Part of me was mad about having to move, the other part was happy to go to a better place.

Now that I'm here, I miss talking on the street without having to remember what the English word is. I miss going to my family and friends' houses, going to parties. At my grandmother's house, she would put down a long, long mat, and many families would sit on the floor together and eat. Here we sit at tables, and only a few people can fit around a table. Also, here I don't know how to joke around with kids my age—I don't know the right English.

Here I bought a computer for myself—I can go on the Internet whenever I want. I have a job. In Iran, for one day, if they pay a lot, they pay seven dollars. I make that much in an hour.

My father reminds me about my promise whenever I do something wrong. He says, "Remember what you said in Iran. What are you doing now?" I say, "OK, Baba, I'm going to go study."

Last year when my mother came to Portland High for parent-teacher conferences, afterwards, when we were walking out, she kissed my cheek and said, "You had trouble in school in Iran, you used to walk with your head down, but now you can hold your head up high. I'm proud of you." That made me feel very good.

Sometimes, here in Portland, we play soccer with all the Iranians. Some are Bahá'i, others are Muslim, but they don't like the Islam of Iran, so they come here. They don't look down on us, they are the same as us.

I don't want anyone to think I hate Muslims. In Iran, the government takes money from Muslims. If you're Bahá'ians, they can't take any away. That's why they push Bahá'ians out or they push Islam on all Bahá'ians.

My religion believes that Muslims and Christians should come together; a thousand years ago there needed to be religious divisions, but now we don't need them anymore. We Bahá'ians don't believe in fighting to convert people to Bahá'i, we just talk to them. Some Muslims still want to fight to convert people, like they did a thousand years ago.

But Muslims believe in God, and Bahá'ians do, too. Most things are the same, except for a few differences. I'm happy I was born Bahá'ian. If I was born into a Muslim family, maybe I'd be one of the people being bad to Bahá'ians in Iran. I'm just trying to be a good person.

Before I left, my Bahá'ian teacher told me, "You're going to be more free than anyone here. Try to be a good person, and tell people about Bahá'i." I made another promise. That's one reason why I want to tell this story. Maybe somebody reads it and finds out about Bahá'i. Not many people here know about my religion.

Untitled

Abdiaziz Mohemud

My name is Abdiaziz Mohamed. I was born in Somalia.

I want to tell my story in case there is someone who thinks they can't learn how to make it. Listen: when I came to Portland, I didn't understand anything. My English was zero. I had no friends.

I tried to get a job at a KFC soon after I arrived. A guy interviewed me. "If I hire you, will you work hard?" he asked.

"No," I said.

He said it again. "If I hire you, will you work hard?"

"No," I said, because I didn't understand what he was saying.

"Okay," he said. "I'll call you back later."

I think he put my application in the trash.

The first time I went to school, real school—not elementary school in Somalia where we played games—was in Portland. I arrived in America in May 2004 with my grandmother, brothers, sisters and cousins. I spoke Somali and Swahili. No English. In September I started school.

When we lived in Nairobi, we didn't have enough money for me to go to school. I looked after my neighbor's trucks. He had several trucks for transporting oil, food and other things. At first I kept an eye on the trucks for him so no one would break into them.

My neighbor drove his trucks to Mombasa, Tanzania, all over. He took me on three trips. I went to Rwanda with him. On one trip we had two flat tires and I helped him fix them. At that time, I thought I wanted to become a truck driver.

I had a lot of friends in Nairobi. They might never see me again.

"Are you going to come back to Kenya?" my friend, Ali, asked before I left.

"I don't know," I said. "The United States is far away and I'm going to start a new life."

After trying to get the job at KFC, I got a job in a factory making cardboard boxes. That job wasn't hard. Dealing with people, that was hard.

I got another job working in a warehouse helping to load food onto trucks for supermarkets. My English was still not very good, but I understood what people said. Tractor trailers came to the warehouse with orders to take to stores all over. We used a machine to take the orders. I punched in my name and badge number and the machine would tell me what products to pick up and which aisle they were in. I took the boxes and crates to the loading dock. I was getting $12 an hour. Then after three months they hired me to load the trucks. That was $15 an hour.

I worked there for seven months but I got sick and had to go to the hospital. The problem was the warehouse was kept cold for the food. It was freezing. I had to stop working there. I got another job cleaning an office building. I work four hours a day after school.

I like school. I feel that I can learn things, and that I can get help in learning. There's not a class I don't like, but my favorites are English, math and history. We're learning American history now. I want to learn all the world's history and about computers, too.

For me, the details of where you are – like the kind of weather, if it's hot or cold – aren't important. What's important is understanding where you live, figuring out how to survive and working to move forward.

.

Four Stories

Hashim Abdi

1. Friends

I'd like to tell you about two friends who lived together, when we were all living in Nairobi. The two friends stuck up for each other and were very close. You'd either find them together or not so far apart from each other. They were mostly just two teenagers I met through other friends. They had just dropped out of school, but they were good guys. You could trust them. But they did drugs. I tried not to be with them because my mother would see me with them. We would play soccer—everyone liked them. People liked to be around them. They lived together and were free most of the time because they didn't go to school.

If I wanted to be in touch with them today, I don't even know where I would start, unless I were to go back to Nairobi. It doesn't really bother me, but I think so often about them and think, "My friends...." Well, I'll make new friends maybe.

Anyway, back then, there ended up being small-scale riots. One particular scuffle took place in South 'B' between two groups (Muslims and Christians) who had some misunderstandings between them. At that time I wasn't in the country. I was told about it by someone who saw it in the newspaper, which I later saw for myself.

The riots turned into a mob and clearly a mob does things senselessly. One of my two friends was involved, and he was telling me how they were messing everything up, breaking car windows. He really had nothing to do with it, but it was there in his neighborhood, and he just jumped in; I guess he felt like acting crazy. He started doing what the people were doing. I can understand why he got involved, though. If you see two groups of people on the streets throwing stones and fighting, destroying property, and you are a male teenager you would want to get involved because of the pressure. If I were there I would have, too. At the time I don't think the two groups knew what it would result in. No one had a clue that the riot police would be called in. It just got out of hand and the mob acted for them.

In the end, my friend got the worst of things. When I came back from vacation, he always talked about his injury from the unrest and how he came to know he was in the hospital and not dead. There is a Swahili proverb that states, "Mtoto akililia wenbe mpe." Literally, it means, "If a child cries for a razor give it to him." What it means is that if someone longs for, or wants to do something, let him do it. It may result in good or bad consequences. For my friend, it went bad in the end—he was hit in the head. He woke up and thought he died, but he was in the hospital. He has a scar on his head that was still there last time I saw him.

2. Nairobi and Portland

In Nairobi, I kind of felt safe. To me, it just felt good, safe there, even if it's not really safe. And here, in Portland, I feel safe, but it's another feeling, something else. Most of the people I knew there were friendly people, and there was a lot of social interaction with people, unlike here.

Here I don't really get to meet people, and I don't really want to. Nairobi neighborhoods had soccer fields, and more than fifty people would go there to meet people, to play and have fun, and do whatever you go there to do. You would just go; you wouldn't know if you'd know anyone when you got there, and it wouldn't matter. Then you'd leave when you were feeling good and had fun. The people were good and welcoming. People met—we had the afternoons together always. People used to go there at four or five and leave at sundown. The mosque had speakers calling people for prayer at that time. Mostly, there was a lot more community. You would just walk a few blocks. People didn't know you, but people would say 'hi,' even if they didn't know you. But here most people...you just pass each other without even signaling hi. There you might just lift a hand, but it was enough.

3. Arriving in a Storm

I was finishing middle school, and I was in my first year of high school in Nairobi. I really wanted to stay there, and then all of the sudden we left. I was like, "Oh well, what can I do? We ended up coming here. My aunt was here already. I told my friends, and they said only, "Oh well, then. Good luck." My first few days, I really didn't know anyone in my neighborhood. I was put in a house on Ocean Ave. My first few days I was just inside. I took a walk with my brother. Whenever we go to new places, other towns, we leave the house and walk, try to figure out the streets or teach ourselves where everything is. Our first night, we walked from Ocean Ave to near USM on Forest Avenue. Then we realized, "Oh, it's getting dark, and we actually don't know where we are."

It was winter and it was snowing. It was a snowstorm and school was out. We knew we'd be coming to Deering High School when we started school, and we had a map, so we started walking. We got lost, just going through those side streets off Woodford Street. I saw a church and it was on the map. We actually found a place to help locate us. Then it was kind of fun. All the roads were icy and there was a lot of snow. We had never been in snow before. We'd seen it before, in the mountains away from Nairobi--like the Boston-Portland distance. Maybe it would snow once in a while, but it wasn't any big snowstorm like that one. And so, we were lost, like you don't know where you are, but you're trying to find a way.

4. An Interview

Interviewer: So technically you're not a refugee; you did not have to leave your country because of war.

Hashim: My father was from Somalia. I was born there. But I've been in Kenya for so long.

Interviewer: So your parents were refugees from Somalia to Kenya.

Hashim: My father actually never made it to Kenya. He was going to Kenya but he died, or something like that.

Interviewer: So you don't know his story?

Hashim: No.

Interviewer: Is that hard for you? Did you know him?

Hashim: I can't really say I knew him. I was like three years old, and I can't actually remember anything about him. So he doesn't actually...I don't really think about it a lot because I never knew him.

Interviewer: So he never made it to Kenya.

Hashim: Well, he went to Kenya, and he came back to get my mother, and we moved to Kenya, and he was supposed to help my uncle, and then I don't know what happened.

Interviewer: So who else came with you?

Hashim: My mom and my three brothers.

Interviewer: So do you consider yourself a refugee?

Hashim: I don't know.

Interviewer: The way I understand it is a refugee is somebody who has to leave his or her country because things are so bad, because of some kind of conflict. But that's not the way you felt about Kenya.

Hashim: Kenya…I never really had to leave there.

Interviewer: Did you think you'd be in Kenya a short time?

Hashim: I really thought I'd be there after high school, and I'd just stay there.

Interviewer: How old were you when you went to Kenya?

Hashim: Around two, less than two years old.

Interviewer: So it was really your home.

Hashim: I consider Kenya home more than Somalia.

Interviewer: Do you think you'll go back there?

Hashim: Sure.

Interviewer: After college?

Hashim: After, maybe.

Interviewer: Would you stay here for college?

Hashim: Well, let's say someone comes here with a degree from any other country — South American, European, African countries or whatever — and they come to get a job in the US, they won't just get the job like this. They have to go back to school. I knew a lot people who did that, and they were like, Sorry you never went to any accredited American school. If you go to college here, and you go to other places in the world, you'll get a job quickly; they think American schools give you a good education.

Interviewer: I imagine your mom would like you to be here longer than college.

Hashim: She wants to leave, to [go back to Kenya], but my aunt was here. She arranged us to come here, so we came.

Interviewer: Is your aunt here by herself?

Hashim: No, she has a family and her mother, my grandmother.

Interviewer: How does your grandmother like it?

Hashim: She's OK, but she doesn't really like it here. She's alone here; she just stays in her house all day. She went to Somalia and Kenya some months ago, and she liked it.

Interviewer: What's it like to pick up and leave and leave everything? What things were you looking forward to about it?

Hashim: Coming to the U.S. Going to school here. Living here. But it's not like I really wanted to come here.

Interviewer: How did your friends in Nairobi take it?

Hashim: They were like, "See you, man, good luck."

Ridwan Hassan

Travels

Ridwan Hassan

I was born in Somalia, in the village of Boohodle, a small place, maybe a couple hundred people. I lived with my Ayeyo, my grandmother, my mother's mother, and my mother's sisters: Nimco, Rodo, Deqa, Halima, Ramla, and Sahra. So many you had to count them on your fingers! I used to play with Sahra, the youngest one. We used to play tag inside the house.

I remember my Ayeyo. She was nice to me. She loved me. She was skinny. Not tall and not short. She wore a dirac—a long dress that went to her feet—and a garabasar—a scarf that she wore around her head. We had a geel, a camel with one hump, that belonged to my Awawe, my grandfather. We used it for riding into Boohodle. You could also milk it—to drink the milk or to make cheese. We also had sheep and goats, two hundred sheep, two hundred goats—a lot. And they lived together and they all slept together in a barn. We also ate the sheep and goats.

There were a lot of people my age in the village. There was a kid named Ahmed, he lived in the same neighborhood. I don't know what he's up to now. I don't keep up with him.

I left there at eight or nine. At that time, my dad and I left for Hargaysa, the capital of Somalia, on our way to go to Kenya. On our way to Kenya, we lived in hotels. My dad asked me to buy some tea. When I got to the store, they had tea, coffee, and food. I bought the tea and tried to go back to the hotel. But when I was crossing the street, a car hit me. My dad saw what happened. It was an old man driving a van who hit me. He got out and put me in the car and drove me to the hospital. I don't remember what happened. In the hospital, when I woke up, my arm was bandaged up. I had broken it in the accident. My dad asked me, "Are you OK?"

Now I know to look around when I am crossing the street.

***

When I was ten or eleven, I went with an auntie, not a real aunt, but a relative, to Jigjigo, in Ethiopia. I lived with her in her house. There were a lot of kids my age. I liked it. We were on our way to Dubai, but we had to stay in Ethiopia for two weeks because I got sick with busbus, the chicken pox. I had a bad case. We couldn't travel because I got sick and then auntie got sick. Female problems. She is in her forties, but couldn't have a baby. She had two sisters and it was their kids who lived with us.

Then we went to Dubai, U.A.E. I had to go with my aunt wherever she went, because she was sick. Dubai was beautiful, like New York, a lot of tall buildings. There were a lot of people who spoke Arabic, different from the Arabic Saudis speak. There's a lot of desert in Dubai. I liked it there. I didn't go to school there; I stayed at home with my aunt and her husband. Sleep, eat, watch TV, sleep again, that's what I did. I never went outside. I did once, with my uncle, but not by myself because I didn't want to get lost. It was a big city and I was little. About twelve, I think.

After six months, I returned with my aunt to Somalia, to Galkayo, a big city, like Portland. There are two types of Somalian people: Hawiye and Dorod. I am Dorod. They were fighting each other every day. I don't know why, but they always fight. That's why Somalia never has a government. They always fight for no reason. Guns and blowing up cars and each other. I wasn't scared. It happens every day, so you get used to it. Dubai was quiet by comparison. No gun sounds. No Pow! I don't even remember the first time I heard a gun or a bomb.

One day, in the town, downtown, we were at school and we heard a car accident in the street. They took the people out—two guys, in their thirties, driving a truck—they didn't have eyes. They were alive, but everything was gone—no teeth, no eyes.

All of us ran to the hospital, about fifteen kids in all. Probably as far as from PHS to Maine Med.

About five of us told the nurses' station, "Maybe he's my dad! Let me see!", because they wouldn't let you in unless you were family. So they let us in. Then we saw them. They were alive, breathing, but all bloody, all over their body.

Then we said, "It's not my dad. It's not my dad." And we left and went back to school. We just did it for fun.

My mom moved from Somalia when I was four. She went to Kenya. I have no idea why she moved. I hadn't seen my mother for a long time, so when I was about fifteen, I decided to go to see her. She was in a refugee camp in Uganda, called Nakivali, about an hour's drive outside Abarara, a big town. I took a plane to Kenya; my mom came from the refugee camp to Kenya to pick me up. I don't know how she got there. The bus, maybe. We took the bus back. It was one night's travel and the bus was full. My mom told me about the camp, how it was. She told me that the camp was like a big town. Forty miles this way, forty miles that way. Not only Somalians lived there; people were from all different countries: Rwanda, Somalia, Congo, Sudan, Burundi. The people stayed apart from each other because they didn't know each other and didn't understand each other. My mother lived in a house she had built for herself. The house was made of wood on the inside, with sand and water mixed on the outside. The roof was made of the same material as an umbrella. She had five kids—all born in the camp. She had been there for nine years, maybe more than that. She was living with my step-dad, step-sister and four sisters and brothers: Samira and Zakaria, eight-year-old twins; Sofia, seven; Daqa, four; and Sahara, ten. They are all younger than me. I get along well with them.

This was in December of 2004 and it was hot. I went to school there. There were all types of kids—all the kids from the refugee camp—all from different countries. We went to the same school. They all spoke different languages, so we used to speak Swahili since everybody speaks Swahili. It's like English. The language belongs to Kenya, but everyone speaks it. It is the common language of East Africa. Everybody speaks it and everybody understands it. But they have their own language, too.

The teachers spoke and wrote English, but some of them spoke Swahili, too. The teachers were from different countries but they were all African. I went to school Monday through Friday 8 a.m to 2 p.m., very much like the schedule here. The teachers had textbooks but the students only had notebooks. The school was eight rooms and every room was its own class. The school started with the age of ten up to any age. Even someone of twenty, twenty-five, or even twenty-nine could go. In Africa, the schools don't care about age. We had a lot of older people in our school. It's good. My favorite class was Math, just like here.

After school, we'd play soccer in a big field. There were white people, Canadians, who used to give us soccer balls. I'm good at soccer. I can play every position. They would pass the ball to me to score. I was good at making goals. This year at PHS, the coach has asked me to play for the school. I'll try. I don't have time for it now, but maybe by the summer I'll get to.

There are three brothers I knew from the camp, who live in the U.S. now, too. Sometimes on Saturdays and Sundays they call me and we talk. They like living here. I used to skip school with them to go play soccer. Also, we had a lake and we used to go swim. It was a long lake where people could fish. Sometimes I went fishing, but we always used to swim. It was kind of dangerous because there were a lot of crocodiles, but we didn't care about them. Kids are crazy.

We flew from Uganda to Utah. The U.S. government helped us to get there. It was last January. I was sixteen. The airport in New Jersey was big. This African lady who was from Kenya spoke Swahili to us and helped us to go to the place where we were supposed to be living. She had a sign with our name on it. We took a plane from NJ to Dallas, and then from Dallas to Utah. A lady was waiting for us there, too. She was our caseworker. We went to a hotel and lived there for a week, and then we found an apartment. I didn't like the food and it was too cold. My step-dad's daughter, Mulki, and I went outside to walk. There was snow, and we could only be outside for five or ten minutes. It was too cold! After about one month, I went to school, to high school, in the 10th grade.

Salt Lake City is a big city. It's like Maine. Bigger than Portland, big like the whole state. There were a lot of mountains—all around the city. I had seen mountains in Somalia but I had only seen snow on TV.

In the beginning, I only ate bread and drank drinks.

When I first ate the chicken, I was about to be sick. I didn't like it. Now chicken is my favorite.

My mom had heard about Maine. I wasn't real interested. They had heard it was quieter. I don't think of it as quiet; it's the same as other states. I like Utah better. I liked the school. I had a lot of friends. I made a lot of friends in four months. I use MySpace to keep up with them. I use it every day. You can see if your friends are online and then you can email them.

I've made friends here at school. I go to the YMCA and play basketball and work out. Sometimes I use the pool. On Saturdays, sometimes I go to the library. I live near the Reiche School on the West End.

On January 14th, my Dad went to Africa, but he is coming back this summer. I may go to Minnesota, where he lives now, to see him. My dad has five kids, all older than me, three girls and three boys. My dad's daughters live in Canada, England, and Saudi Arabia. Only the brothers live in the U.S. Maybe when I get my passport I'll go see them. I like traveling. I would like to go everywhere. I will go to Europe and Canada. I haven't seen my dad since I was nine, the year I broke my arm, when we were on our way to Kenya. It has been so long, I can't even remember which arm I broke.

Guy Stuff

Estella Omal

When we lived in Sudan, my three brothers played soccer, but I wasn't allowed. I think it's against the law down there. Girls are not allowed to do anything. Only the guys. My mom and grandma were like, "Why you doing guy stuff?" Girls could play hopscotch and jump rope, and I watched TV. Sometimes I had to clean, but not that much because I have two older sisters.

When no older people were home, I would play soccer with my brothers. Sometimes one of my sisters and a female cousin would play, too. I like to play soccer because I like running around. We would play on the dirt road in front of our house. Or in our yard, which had a hard surface, sort of like a patio. Outside of the yard, the ground was sandy. We got really dirty playing there because of the sand, and sometimes we kicked rocks by accident. My brothers, especially my little brother, were better at soccer than me, maybe because they got to play more. I never worried about someone seeing us play and telling on me. We never got caught.

We lived with my grandma instead of my mom. I never met my dad. When I was about seven, I went to live with my aunt. She had a new baby, and she needed help. They lived far away. One of my sisters went to live with my uncle and his wife to help with their baby. My mom died when I was about eight.

When I was ten, my family left Sudan so my oldest brother wouldn't have to fight in the war. My grandma, my two sisters, two of my brothers, my aunt, her six children and I took a train and then a boat to Egypt. My oldest brother went to Egypt before us. I was sad to leave our house. I cried a little bit. The boat trip took a day and a half. It was fun. People fished from the boat. We moved to Cairo. I went to an all-black school. There was a soccer field at the school, but only boys played there. But then my aunt found out about a girl's soccer team at her church. She went to a different church than me because she is not a Catholic. My cousin told me, "There's soccer going on, go sign up."

My grandma was in charge of the family, but I thought she would tell me I couldn't play. She thought, "If you're not a guy, then you better just go inside the house and look for something to do, not play soccer outside." Instead I asked my older sister if I could play. She said OK. My grandma never said anything.

It was fun to play. I didn't get to play in the games, though, because the other girls went to a different school than me. I had school on game days. The other girls on the team were from all over Africa, including Sudan. I wore shorts to play soccer even though the white women in Egypt weren't allowed to wear shorts or short skirts. You cannot play soccer with pants or sweatpants; you need to play in shorts.

I play wing. I help with defense. That's my thing. I also help other players make goals, but I don't try to make them myself. I pass the ball. Being up near the goal scares me. I try to understand why, but I can't. The wing helps at your goal and then runs all the way down to the other goal to help there. You need to be fast.

I only got to play soccer for one year in Egypt. Then there was stuff I needed to do at home. My sister was working. And my grandma was staying home, so I tried to help her.

I knew my family was trying to move to the United States, but I only found out we were going for sure two weeks ahead of time. I wanted to stay in Egypt. I had friends there, and I was worried about learning English. I was in eighth grade when we moved here. There are a lot of nice people here, but I think Portland is too quiet. I like to be in noisy places because I make a lot of noise. I like screaming and laughing and jumping around. People here are quiet. And there's too much snow.

I live with my grandma, two of my brothers, and one of my sisters. My oldest brother died in a car accident in Maine about a year ago. My older sister is married and has a one-year-old named Colin. She lives with her husband.

When we first moved here, I played tennis for a couple of years instead of soccer, but then it got boring. At first I couldn't play soccer because I had to baby-sit for my nephew after school while my sister worked. Now my little brother, Walter, baby-sits. I tell him, you baby-sit, and then later if I come, you ask anything, I will do it. Because if I don't go to practice, I cannot play. And then I go home, and he says, "Do this. No, no. Take this upstairs. No, bring it back." I cook for him, but he won't eat macaroni and cheese, which is my favorite thing to eat. I make fried eggs for him. I like baby-sitting when I don't have anything else to do. I like to watch my nephew do stupid stuff and fall down. I laugh at him.

I played in my first real soccer game last summer. Our home field is by Back Bay, and it's not as hot or dirty playing here as in Africa. We play for fifteen minutes at a time and then rotate. I cannot just keep running and running and running. I get out of breath. But everyone plays at least once in the first and second halves of each game.

The games are fun, but I am the only black person. I used to play with only black people. I wasn't used to playing with all white people. There is a black American on the team, but she doesn't have black, black skin color like me. I have fun with my teammates. They don't think it's weird that I'm the only African, but I do. After a while my cousin joined the team. And then she quit. She left me by myself again. There are a lot of blacks on the boy's team, but a lot of the girls run track instead. Maybe next year there will be another black person.

The Dogs

Hamid Karimian

It was a regular day, not too hot, and not cold at all. I was walking home with my best friend Hemin from school. We were both in 5th grade. I was a year older than him, he was ten and I was eleven years old. We had a lot in common and had been friends since kindergarten. We didn't live too far away from each other, just across the street I could spot his bedroom window from my house. Every day after school we would race to the sandwich store, so we would be really hungry by the time we got there. As we entered the store, we could smell the different types of sandwiches being cooked; the chicken sandwich with pickles, grilled steak, and our favorite, the macaroni sandwich. For some odd reason we were addicted to that sandwich. It was affordable and very tasty. We were regular customers in that store, so that automatically earned us free drinks.

After our lunch we would walk around for a while, then head home. My dad was never home, so Hemin would usually come to my house to watch TV. When we got bored, we went outside and played soccer with other kids, hide and seek, and all kinds of other games that we made up. Homework was always our last priority-- we never cared for it that much. I managed to keep my grades in a good shape, but Hemin was failing badly. I tried to help him, but he was never paid attention, so I finally gave up. That school year went by really quick and it was almost summer. Me and Hemin had planned to save some money to buy a mountain bike. It wasn't that expensive, but it would take us a while to save up for that, so that meant no more spending money on sandwiches and candy. It didn't actually take that long to come up with the money; I guess Hemin's dad had decided to give him some money and that was all we needed.

It was a great summer for us, even though we only had one bike. We would take turns riding it, but we were both on the bike at all times. We went swimming at the falls, went to parks, and just spent almost every minute of that summer together. Towards the end of the summer, my dad told me that it was financially hard for him to feed me and his new wife together, so he was gonna let me go back to my mother, who had migrated to America and was also remarried. He told me all the stuff about how much he loved me and how hard it was for him to see me go away, but I knew those words weren't coming from his heart. He had suffered me for years and banned me from seeing my own mother, and now he was telling me he loved me. That day I was so happy, and I just couldn't believe that I was finally going back to my mom. I had dreamed of this day since I was five years old, and finally it came.

I was twelve years old now and had already started in a new school in sixth grade. Hemin was also in that school and we had almost every class together. I had told him about going to America to my mom, but he didn't believe me. That year was no different than other years. We continued our daily routine: I would wake up early in the morning, walk over to his house and throw a rock at his window to wake him up. We walked over to a milk shop where they had fresh milk. We bought a cup and drank it fast so we wouldn't be late to school. On our way to school there were a couple of alley dogs that would start barking and chase us for a quarter of a mile, but we always beat them. On our way back from school, we'd stop at the sandwich store, and then go home to play soccer and fool around all day.

It was towards the end of the year. My mom had hired smugglers to bring me from Iraq to Turkey where the UN would take care of me and bring me to my mom after a while. One day as we were walking back from school, I told Hemin that next week I was leaving. He immediately knew I wasn't playing around, and I saw the big frown on his face. We stopped at the sandwich store that day, but he didn't eat his sandwich. I knew it was hard for him and for me, but it was a better future for me and I couldn't miss that chance.

My last day was sad. I felt like I lost something big in my life, and I know Hemin felt the same way, too. I promised him that I would stay in touch with him and he would always remain my best friend. We had shared happiness and sadness together and always looked out for one another. I could not forget him just like that. I gave him everything that I wasn't able to bring with me, and he gave me a couple things so that would remember him.

That day my dad drove me to a bigger city where I would meet the manager of the smugglers who would take me from there. We stayed in the city for a night, and the next day we went to find the manager. He owned a crystal store where they sold expensive house utensils. The manager seemed very nice and caring, but you could never trust them. My dad had no choice, and I just wanted to go away from him and accepted the consequences of my trip. When it was time for me and my dad to split off, he started crying, and that image always remains in my head. I had never seen him so helpless before, and he gave me kiss on my forehead. I gave him my watch, mainly because he didn't have one and because I wanted to show him that even though he was never a good father to me, I cared for him and was going to miss him a lot.

The manager handed me over to a couple of guys and they drove me to a village where I would meet the smuggler who would take me to Turkey. As soon as we arrived there, five dogs were chasing us because we weren't familiar to them. Two young boys came to greet me, one of them about my size. Then a young tall man came out of the house and happily greeted me. I figured he was the smuggler. He was in his twenties, and a very sharp-looking man. Then after him, his mother came out; I figured she was about 70 years old. She had an arc-shaped back, but walked as if she was in her 30's. They had an old dog that was lying down by their door, he didn't move anything but his head.

The village was very green and located in a mountain range area. Their house was exactly on top of the biggest hill in the village. It was a house made out of mud and rocks. No formal bedrooms or kitchen, it was all one big room. They had their kitchen set up in a corner of the room, beddings on one side, and the rest of the space to sit. They didn't have a bathroom, the nearest one was about a hundred yards away from their house. They owned some animals, chickens, goats, cows, donkeys, and some snakes. They were a very nice family, and they welcomed me warmly.

That night I wasn't very comfortable and nervous. The smuggler came over to me and told me that we were going to leave the next day, and that I shouldn't be scared of anything and think of them as my friends. They fed me pretty good that night. I had chicken with rice and some other foods that I had never tried before. I liked them, and I didn't hesitate while I was eating. The next day when I woke up, breakfast was ready. Fresh milk from their cows, cheese, yogurt, fresh eggs, honey, fresh baked bread, and lots more. I was truly in heaven with all that food waiting for me to dig in.

After breakfast, I went out with the kids to play. They warned me about a very dangerous dog that lived nearby. They said he had killed a couple of strangers already. That scared the crap out of me, so I tried to look out for dogs as much as possible. We ran around playing hide and seek and other games. I met some new kids and we all went out donkey hunting. We found some and jumped on top of them so that we could ride them. Later, the smuggler came and told me that we weren't leaving that night. A man had been shot with his horse trying to smuggle some alcohol over the border, and it wasn't safe for us to leave that night. So I was stuck there until they were sure that the ways were totally clear.

That afternoon, I was sitting on top of the hill looking over the village, dreaming about coming to America and what my life was going to be like. I was thinking about having a nice car, going to school with girls and all my fantasies would come true. I was deep in my thoughts when I heard something breathing really hard behind me, I slowly turned my head, and there it was, the killer dog. I didn't take a second to think about what I was going to do; I started running down the hill as fast as I could. The dog chased me for a couple of seconds and then stopped, but I was still running. At a point I tripped over a rock and started rolling down the hill. I was all dirty and muddy by the time I had stopped rolling. The dog was looking at me from the top of the hill like I was stupid or something. So I got up and walked to find someone that could help me walk back to the house without the dog chasing me.

I stayed at the village for about a week, and then it was time to go. The word was that the ways were safe. I packed my things and tried them up to the horse. I said my thanks and goodbyes to the family for taking care of me that week. The smuggler told me it was going to be a long, cold trip.

There was snow on the mountains, and in some places we had to walk and pull the horses. We were off on our way by six clock that evening and it would take us six to eight hours to get to Turkey, depending on the road conditions. I was on the horse most of the way. In some places, like he said, we had to pull the horse up the mountains in the deep snow. I was wearing two pairs of wool socks, boots, and all kinds of warm layers and jacket, but I was still freezing. I couldn't feel my hands and toes any more. I fell asleep a little on the way when the horse wasn't running.

The border patrol was visible in some parts, and thank god, they never saw us. We arrived at a village in Turkey at about three o'clock in the morning. I was very tired and cold. The smuggler took me to a house; there was a man waiting for me at the door. He helped me get off the horse and carried in my luggage for me. The smuggler gave me a hug and told me that from here this family would take care of me and get me to my destination. He didn't stay and took off very quickly.

The man took me inside the house and he asked if I was hungry. I told him I was really sleepy and just wanted to rest. He gave me a pillow and a blanket and I fell asleep very quickly. The next morning, he came and woke me up. He told me to have some breakfast quickly because he was taking me to another village. After breakfast, there was a car waiting for me outside the house. I got in and the driver didn't say anything to me the whole way. It was about a twenty minute trip to that village. When we arrived at the village, an elderly man greeted me, but I couldn't understand a word he was saying. He spoke Turkish, and I didn't know any.

I was there for two days. I didn't really do much because I could not communicate with them. I just told them in sign language if I was hungry. After the two days, I got into a car again, and I was off on my way to Van, the city where I was to meet with my mom's cousin. When I got there, the smugglers manager had another store in

Turkey, but a phone card store, not crystals. He wasn't there himself but another guy that spoke my language. He told me that my mom's cousin, Yousef, would come any minute to pick me up, and he did. I was so happy to see him. I had known him since I was a kid, and I felt comfortable with him. On our way back to his house he asked me about the trip, and I told him from the start to the end.

I stayed in Turkey for nine months, and I faced the same problems that I had been facing all my life: dogs. Those Turkish dogs were even worse than the ones at my place! They chased you until you found a place to hide. I hated them, that's why I didn't go out at night too much. Other than the dogs, I had a pretty basic life. I lived with my aunt and her husband for the time being and they took care of me as their own child.

After the nine months were over, I flew to New York. I didn't speak a word of English, and I didn't know what was going on. All I knew was that I was coming to my mom and had to trust the people that were guiding me this whole time. I switched airports in New York. On the way to the other airport, I saw people walking with dogs, and the dogs weren't chasing anyone. They behaved very well and looked intelligent. After a while in New York, I flew over here to Portland where I reunited with my mom. It was a night I'll always remember.

Trouble Walking

Farah Jama

Today I am having trouble walking. My knee is hurting me because yesterday, Sunday, I was playing soccer with my team and was kicked by another boy. My coach said it was not necessary for me to go to the doctor, that I should put ice on it and not play for two weeks. This will be very hard because I like to be with my friends and play soccer with them on the weekends. My father was a soccer coach, and when I was a little boy in Mogadishu, Somalia, he taught me and my brothers how to play.

There was not much to do in Kakuma, the refugee camp in Kenya where we went when I was eleven, so my older brother and I played a lot of soccer. There were no teams at the camp, and we had only each other to play with. Now he lives in Canada where he is in college. He is a champion soccer player. He will go to Brazil next month to play a match there. I have lost my papers that would allow me to leave the country to play soccer in other places, so I cannot do this.

I lived in the refugee camp for four years. It was called "Kakuma 1." Later, after more people came, there were Kakuma 2, 3 and 4. It was not a safe place. I was there with my mother, my sister and my brother. My father was there at first, but after a year he left to go back to Somalia. There was little food and we ate only once a day. Mostly we ate rice and sometimes a little goat meat. We had to prepare our own meals and be sure we didn't lose our ration cards. I had a friend there. One day he said he was going to go outside the camps to look at the wild animals. He liked to watch them for he found them beautiful. I told him not to go. Not to go. I said, "It is dangerous outside the camp and the lions will eat you." But he did not listen to me. He said, "Don't worry, Farah, I will be safe." He went out into the jungle, and he never came back. I think the lions ate him. After that I didn't have a friend to play with.

After four years in the camp, my sister got very sick. A scorpion bit her hand, and it did not heal. My mother tried to get medical help for her, but she could not get it because of the police. The police say they will take you to a doctor if you give them money. But if you give them money they will not take you to the doctor, they will take the money and you will never see them again.

This upset my mother very much. Finally, she got some money from her brother so that we could leave the camps to find a doctor for my sister. She paid a farmer with a tractor to take us to Nairobi, the capital of Kenya. The four of us rode on the tractor for four days until we came to the city. It rained the whole time we were riding on the tractor. When we got there, a friend of my mother's arranged for us to have a place to stay in an apartment house. My mother was able to take my sister to the doctor. My sister got well and is still well today.

When I got hurt playing soccer yesterday, I didn't worry because I knew that if I needed to, I could go to a doctor without having to bribe the police. I want people in Portland to know how bad the police are in Kenya, and I want them to know that the police here in Portland are helping the people. One day, I was outside, and a boy came up to me and started a fight. We were fighting and fighting, and I couldn't make him stop. I had my cell phone, and I called 911. The police came and made the other boy stop fighting me. This would not have happened in the camp. No one would have come. Every morning in the camps I would wake up and find that people had been killed in the night: Sometimes as many as twenty people were killed in one night. Mostly it was the women who were killed. Here, this is not happening so much because the police are keeping us safe.

While I was in the camp, I was thinking that I would some day go home and see my father again. After we left Nairobi we were able to go back to Mogadishu, but my father did not come to visit me. I was asking and asking my mother where my father was. I was bored at home and wanted my father to come and take me swimming like he always did. At first, she said he was working and could not come today, but when he did not come for a long time I began to think she was lying to me. Finally, I said to my brother, "Tell me what happened to our father." And he told me. He told me that my father had been killed two years ago in the Civil War. Soon after this we left for America.

Some people ask me about my future. I tell them, "When I get out of high school do you know what I want to be? I want to be a policeman." I want to be an honest policeman who helps people stay out of fights. And if someone needs to go to the hospital, I want to be able to take them there so they can get cured. But what I want now is for my knee to get better fast so next Sunday I can play soccer with my friends.

Mohamed Rashid Isaack

Family

Mohamed Rashid Isaack

I am seventeen years old, and my name is Mohamed Rashid Yussuf Sharif Isaack. I was born in Somalia in a place called Bardere. Due to the war, my family and I were unable to cope with the situation, which was going from bad to worse day after day.

I remember leaving our farm in the village of Bardere in northern Somalia. I was four years old. On the farm we grew corn, rice, and sugar cane. We had goats, cows, camels, and a donkey named Damer a Dow. Sometimes, when my mom went to the river, she brought the donkey to help bring back the water.

One day men with guns came to our house and they said to my father, "You don't own this farm anymore." My father tried to speak and the men said, "If you talk, you will see something," which meant they would kill him. They gave us time to leave town. We brought some clothes and one of our camels. We brought a small amount of rice and corn.

We were in a refugee camp in the northeast part of Kenya for nine years. Life in the camp was a little bit more comfortable than life in Somalia. I was in middle school when the agency responsible for our refugee status decided on a resettlement process to the U.S. My family was very happy with this announcement. I can recall one of our neighbors cried tears of joy when he heard the incredible news of our resettlement.

After traveling to Nairobi, Amsterdam, and New York City—and sleeping one night on NYC transit—Roanoke, Virgina was our first stop. I went to Patrick Henry High School—there were no Somali students. There were black and white American students only. The students at school made fun of me and mocked the way I spoke. They teased me about my clothes.

The first two weeks I was depressed. I was speaking little English, and the English I knew was British, that is the reason they laughed when I was speaking.

One day some old friends of my father living in the

state of Maine tried to contact him. My father accepted their offer to come to Maine because he knew we would never have friends in Virginia. We arrived in Portland in January, 2006.

My father talked to me one day. He said, "I want you to go to college. You have to work hard, and I will try to pay the money. I will put $150 every month in the bank so that when you finish high school there will be a lot of money, and you will pay for college."

Let me tell you about my family: There are twelve of members in my family. We moved from the same country. We have the same religion and color. We share everything. We are normal people who are in good condition. We hate back-biting people. We hate war. We like to develop the community. We moved from a land of civil war to a peaceful environment. We left behind relatives like my grandmother in Kenya. We didn't involve ourselves in the civil war—the important issue for us was to move to save our lives. We looked for education for our children. We looked for work to be self-sufficient. We wanted to move to a neutral land to achieve all our goals. My family

makes me feel happy. They remind me that togetherness
and brotherhood will never bring betrayal.

The Journey

Jackson Benjamin

I woke up to a sunny morning. It was about 102 degrees; it was so hot, and the ground was so dry, you could see steam rising up. My mother was in the kitchen cleaning and cooking. I quietly came into the room to say good morning to her as she was washing the dishes.

I said, "Good morning. How did you sleep?"

She slowly turned around and said, "Good morning, Gayshe. I slept well, but Mariam's dog kept barking all night long. *Barko, barko, barko*, all night long. But, sit down. Where were you yesterday? I did not see you come in."

"I was in the fields with some friends playing dominoes under the moonlight."

She looked at me. She knew better. She knew I was hanging out in the fields with my friends, with the soldiers, with the girls, with the thieves, with the drunks, with the cards, with the gambling.

She stopped washing the dishes and focused her eyes on me. She asked me, "How do you feel about the Sudanese army?"

I told her, "The army is my future because after I'm done with my studies I plan to serve in the army."

Mother looked at me and said, "I do not want you to die like James, Juma, Juna, and Junas," and she recited name after name.

"What are you trying to say?"

She moved slowly towards me. "We have the chance to go to America and avoid all of this Sudanese nonsense. I want you to have a better future." She stopped and told me to think about it.

I could not understand why we would have to leave our homeland to have a better future. I liked knowing where I was going, what I would be doing. I knew that I would have to finish school, then go to the army, have a family, become a minister. Why would I want to leave behind all my friends and family? Why would I want to leave the fields were Backo and I had fun? Who would play the drums on New Year's if I wasn't here? I would feel guilty not joining Backo and the others in the army. I wanted to defend my country, and hang out in the fields with the boys, and wear the new uniform so the girls would think I looked handsome. Wearing a uniform was like having a million dollars in your pocket. All the girls want you.

What would America bring me? Peace? Freedom? Why would that matter when my future was already promised to me? But then I thought of my sister Samira and my younger brother Marko. Did I want them to die like the names of the boys my mother recited to me or did I want them to go to school? And what about my mother and father? What would their future be like here? Would they be going to funerals when they could be going to graduation days? I came to an understanding that going to America could change all our lives.

That afternoon I ran to my mother and said, "I don't want to join the Sudanese army." She smiled and told me to get her a cup of cold water.

* * *

I woke up with a loud banging noise on the right side door of the train. I opened my eyes slowly and a dark tall man covered with a black cloth stood right above me. He gradually removed the black cloth and said, "Son where is your ticket?" With a hurry I jumped off my seat and started looking for my ticket. All of a sudden, I remembered a time when my uncle William told me he lost his train ticket in Wow, Sudan. He said the ticket collector arrested him and took him to jail, because he was thought to be a "free-loader" and was given a fine of five hundred dollars. As I came back to reality, I realized I needed to find my ticket or I was going to hit the highway and that was not an option. Ooooooooooooh, I remembered I put it inside my right shoe so I wouldn't lose it. I quickly took off my shoe and handed him the ticket. He looked at me with a dark eye and said, "Thank you," and left through the damaged door. I got back on my feet and sat down with ease.

* * *

It was around nine in the morning—the sky was white, the terminal was white. It was filled with so many white people whom I never thought existed in the world. Every man had a suitcase and was wearing a tie, the women looked shiny from head to toe, and wore black dresses with huge coats and pairs of glasses that added taste to their style. Walking out the terminal meant walking out to a new world, a world with no boundaries, with no end to it. The JFK International Airport was like a soccer arena, where all the fans from all over the world would come to cheer on the team they admire the most. At twelve years old it was too much, I took a seat by the gate and closed my eyes and wondered…

Is this real or am I just dreaming? I swear it's a dream that I can't wake up from. It seemed as though it was the night after President Clinton had bombed a hospital. In the news it said that the Sudanese government was in the act of building chemical weapons for Iraq. Everyone in town was amazed by this invisible aircraft that came out of nowhere and let out a few bombs without being seen. It was clear to every citizen that the Americans weren't to be messed with.

* * *

171 Congress St. in Portland, Maine, zip code 04101: my first American address, a three apartment building complex. The first floor white people lived in, the second floor a Somalian family lived in, and the third floor belonged to my family and me. It was located in a pretty calm neighborhood with few little kids. Every morning I would wake up listening to the Portland Fire Department noise, and after that it was all quiet. I did not step out of the house maybe for a few weeks at first. The reason was, I didn't know anybody who lived closed to my house, and plus I didn't know the town very well.

On May 20, 2001, a friend who lived across the street from my house came and knocked on my door and invited me to come and "chill" with him. At first I had no interest in going with him, but I said to myself, "What the hell, I have been in this house too long, I need to get out and meet people," so I did. He first gave me a tour around the downtown area ,which was kind of interesting, it had the

PPL, which stands for Portland Public Library, and I was walking through Time Square.

Around three o'clock we walked down to a neighborhood called KP. I had no idea what KP stands for, but walking down to KP felt like walking back home. Down the street there were people who were speaking Arabic, Zande, and many other African languages. I had the biggest smile, and I felt like crying because it was just like home just in a different environment.

Now I am supposed to be grateful for being here, for being alive, but it is not that simple.

Kahiye Hassan

Ponce de Leon Walk

Kahiye Hassan

It was common for my father and me to take a walk around Portland in those first weeks. We were like Ponce de Leon trying to find the legendary "Fountain of Youth." Our journey started on the October morning we headed out Danforth Street towards the Old Port. I had never seen so many dead leaves lying on the ground. The bright yellows, reds and oranges were like the sun lying on top of the earth. This was very weird to me because the life hadn't been sucked out of the leaves. When I snapped the edge off the stem of a yellow and red leaf, white fluid oozed out. The trees didn't look lifeless either. Their roots were healthy beneath the ground. The grass couldn't be any greener. The ground was moist because it had rained a couple weeks earlier. Not like in Kenya. When it rained there, it rained—for hours, sometimes days. Here the rain was about a five-minute thing, and there wasn't any sign of drought. As my dad and I continued our walk, the first place we came upon was Vespucci's Market, a small grocery store at the corner of Danforth and High. My dad bought me my first bag of chips, Lays. They were crunchy and very oily. I was used to homemade French fries; I had never tasted anything like this before. We left and continued our voyage up High Street. There was a tan mansion with a beautifully landscaped lawn. The fence around the lawn was made of fancy iron. This was my dream house.

"Dad, I want to live there," I said.

"You have to work for it," he replied.

As our mission continued up the street, on our right came the museum. Not knowing it was a museum, I said again, "No, this one is mine."

I remember the wind was blowing hard, smacking me on the left side of my face with the hood of my jacket.

My dad said, " Just like a child has to learn to crawl before he can walk, you have to go through school before you can get that."

We kept going up to Congress Street and went into Paul's Supermarket. I was determined to get sweets:

honey buns, peanut butter, chocolate wafer cookies, and Hostess Sno Balls covered with coconut. This was the closest I could come to finding a real coconut. I was used to seeing coconut trees everywhere in Kenya. I had assumed coconuts and mangoes would always be a part of my life, but this store didn't even have mango juice. It was not at all like the Bakare back in Somalia where there were a bunch of stores, like a yard sale almost, and you could buy spices, clothes, silverware, batteries, boom boxes, and generators all in the same place.

My dad called me over. "Kahiye, come over here. Hold this." He handed me the mesh bag that was filled with bread, eggs, and lettuce. As he walked toward the milk, I saw this familiar jar my cousin introduced me to in Kenya: strawberry jelly. I couldn't believe it! So many other things weren't here, but this long lost taste was sitting right in front of me. Could this be?

When we got home the first thing I took out of the bag was the jar of jelly. I couldn't get it open so I asked my father to help. When he opened the jar there was a loud pop like a champagne cork. The smell radiated through the entire house; the long lost odor alone made me full. Suddenly I was transported back in time to my cousin's house, where I was spoiled with sweets. I just wanted to keep it right there in my hands rather than eating it. I thought it could be a long time before we could buy it again. I stuck my index finger out like a hook and dipped it into the jar. Not wanting to miss a drop I put my mouth over the jar so in case anything spilled it would go right back in.

The taste softened my tongue; the seeds did not interfere with the essence of the flavor or diminish the taste. They were the taste, providing flexibility to the tongue. For days I munched the strawberry jelly from my hidden stash, which I refused to share with anyone, and came up with many ways to eat it rather then sucking it with a spoon. I ate it with Somalian angera, bread, gapaty, and learned later to eat it with peanut butter.

The next day my father and I took the same path into town, but instead of going to the grocery store, we went into the building of Catholic Charities, the group that sponsored us to come to America. We picked up jackets, gloves, mittens, winter hats, and scarves for the upcoming winter. A white woman with short, blond hair took my father to fill out paperwork. I stuck my face into a room full of toys. Boy, did I hit the jackpot. I picked up a fire truck with a long ladder that extended electrically. I was absorbed in a world I had created. I was the architect of my own matrix.

Then I heard a loud sound. When the truck's siren went off, I quickly jumped up, shocked. The white lady came into the room, smiled and said, "I should have known all along this is where he'd be." But my dad's eyebrows escalated, and he stared right through me. It was like in the movie Hercules when Hera's eyes appear up in the sky. I immediately picked up the fire truck and turned it off. I apologized to the lady and followed them out. My father asked me "Why are you always doing things without thinking first?" It was one of his rhetorical questions.

With my new jacket and hat, we started heading back to our house, but took a different path this time. We passed High Street going towards the Longfellow statue and saw Joe's Smoke shop, which seemed just right for my dad. He bought his cigarettes and my first Snickers bar. I was set.

Right next door was the Laundromat. My dad had been looking for a place to wash our clothes, because the weather here was cold and there were not hot breezes for drying. We went inside. My father started reading the signs to operate the washers and dryers, and I just stood there absorbed by the movements of the people. I was good with machines, so I was helping him puzzle out what to do. He was the mind and I was the mechanic. Together we figured everything out.

One night, it just got really cold. My feet and my fingers for the first time were frozen. I went to bed seeing the stars, but the next morning, when I woke up, it looked like someone had covered the ground up in a lustrous blanket, or had a pillow fight. It was still cold. After eating jelly for breakfast, my father and I took our dirty clothes to the laundry. As we walked on this white pearl frosting, it felt like a sponge that didn't keep its shape. The sun reflected on the blanket, making sparks. After we washed our clothes, we headed down State Street toward Danforth Street, and this white, fragile, puffy cotton came tumbling down softly from the sky. I wondered if it was raining, but I couldn't hear it, and I couldn't feel it. It just appeared. The atmosphere was getting warmer. I took my gloves off to reach for it, but it melted on my hand. I stuck my tongue out. It didn't taste how I expected—it was just like water. My dad reached down, picked some up and threw it at me. He sprayed my face and put some more inside my jacket. I jumped up because it was cold—it felt like glitter was under my jacket. I tried to spray him, but it didn't reach. This was how I first learned to make a snowball, pressing it together with my gloves. I tossed the snowball at him, hitting him in the back of his neck.

I liked the snow then because it was new, but now I despise it—it's like a song that got over played.

After a few years in Portland, everything new became old news, and everything that I had done in that first year, I longed for. Life always makes you want something that you can't see, or you can't grasp. As my life changed and became more Americanized, new things no longer impressed me. America is a fast-paced, changing culture, but once you become used to the pace, there are no surprises, like first-time snow. I loved the journeys with my dad in the first days of America, when we walked side by side as one. Those walks are not lost, but waiting to be reborn.

The Faithful Doves of My Father: An Unforgettable Story

Aqila Sharafyar

My father kept birds—about 15 beautiful white doves—behind our house in Kabul. He had them as long as I could remember, from the time I was a very small child. My dad loved the birds, more than anyone else in my family. He was the one who fed them, who cleaned out their cage, which was behind our house and the size of a small room. He would go out and talk to them, making little dove calls as he encouraged them to eat. He also put small bangles around their ankles, which would jingle as they walked. That way we could hear the birds when we were inside the house, cooing and jingling outside while we ate our dinner, or sat and talked as a family in the evenings.

I was very young at the time, maybe six or seven years old, but I loved helping my dad with the birds. I loved the way the cage smelled. I liked going in and helping to sprinkle seeds for them on the floor, or bring them pieces of bread from the house. My older sisters never went into the bird house. But I was always with my dad. Whenever he was doing something, I was always with him. If he were going to a friend's house, I was with him. Some days I would even ride the bus to his work, where he was a manager at a human resources firm. Other days, I'd stay home with my mom and sisters or go to school. On Fridays, my father would go to the mosque to pray. Sometimes, he'd take me with him to the mosque. I never prayed. I just walked around, playing with the water outside of the mosque or looking at my reflections in the mirrors hung all around.

***

When the war started in 1992, our lives changed a lot. My dad stopped going to the mosque, because it was too dangerous to go there. He stopped going to work every day. At first he went every other day, but after a while it was just too dangerous to travel on the roads. He was scared he'd be killed. Even when we were in our house, the bombs were exploding every place, or there were planes dropping bombs. There were different governments in the north and south of our city, and they were shooting each other. It was the Sunni versus the Shia'a. The Sunni mostly spoke Pashtun and the Shia'a mostly spoke Farsi, so they not only were fighting about different languages and different religions, but more than anything, they were fighting over which group would rule the country.

My family is Shia'a, but my school was mixed—Sunni and Shiia kids together. If the teachers were Sunni, they treated the Sunni kids better than they did the others. In Afghanistan, there are more Sunni than Shia'a people. They always had the highest power. My sisters didn't go to school, because they were treated poorly there for being Shia'a, for being a lower class. But I loved school, even though the teachers sometimes hit us with sticks or rulers. Even today, if one of my teachers in the U.S. gets mad, I start shaking and I forget everything.

After the war started, we mostly stopped going to school. A lot of people moved away. Our street got really empty. Every house, every family, wanted to move. A lot of people were going to Pakistan, or to Iran. We stayed in school for a couple of months, but when the war got really bad, my mom wouldn't let us go anymore. I spent my days playing behind our house close to the doves.

Sometimes, it was so dangerous to go out on the streets that we would not get any food. We'd send the men out to climb up into the trees and pick apples for us to eat. When the bombing was bad, all the neighbors would come to my house because we had a basement, and you could hide in there. As the war got worse, everybody came to hide with us. They stayed once for two or three weeks. Everyone was looking for a safer place to live, trying to decide where to go. We all sat in our basement, eating apples and drinking water, and wondering what to do next.

Even during this time, though, my dad went outside to feed his doves. I remember he used to fuss over their feathers. He sometimes used colorful paint—like pink and green—and would put little marks on the heads of his favorite birds, just to make them look prettier. And that jingling sound they made because of the bangles he put on their ankles: he loved to hear that, especially when they were all walking at the same time. It sounded a little like raindrops.

The war continued to get worse, though, and my parents thought we should move closer to the city, where it might be safer for us. My dad did not want to leave the birds, but he also knew that he couldn't bring them with us. We were moving into his sister's house and there was no room there. So my dad sold the doves to a man who lived in a different neighborhood. We didn't sell our house. We just locked the doors and left.

***

In downtown Kabul, things weren't much safer. There were fewer explosions than there had been at the old house, but the Sunni mujahadeen were gathering on the outskirts of the city and it was becoming more dangerous to be downtown. One day my dad traveled back to our house to pick up some of our belongings. When he got there, he found that all of his doves were sitting in our yard or on top of the house, as if they'd been waiting for him to show up. The man who had bought them had left a note on the door for my dad. He wanted his money back because the doves would not stay with him. They only wanted to be back at our house.

We had been living with my aunt for maybe two months by then. The war was just as bad in her neighborhood as it had been in our old neighborhood. My parents were talking about trying to get us to Pakistan, to get out of the country as refugees, but my mom didn't want to. She and my sisters missed the house. My mom said, "We don't want to go to a different country, because we don't have enough money. If we go to Pakistan, we're not going to have food or a house to live, and we're going to die there, too. We've got to go back to our old house.

So we moved back to our home, but something scary happened along the way. We had found a taxi to take us from my aunt's house to our old house. But once we reached our neighborhood, there was a checkpoint. The guards there pulled my dad out of the car and pointed a gun at him, saying that he was Pashtun. The place that we lived, they didn't like Pashtun people and were killing them. My dad said, "No, I'm not Pashtun!" But they didn't believe him. My mom screamed and was crying. We were all crying. Eventually, they let him go and we made it back to the house.

My dad paid the guy who'd bought the doves, so they belonged to him again. At this point most of our neighbors had gone. The streets were mostly empty. There were just a few kids left. I used to be able to hear them playing marbles and shouting playfully outside on the streets, but now it was so quiet. All the doors were locked. There was one family of three people left on the street, good friends of ours. They'd felt afraid living on that lonely street, and soon they moved into the lower floor of our house. We were so happy to be back home, to be back with the doves. We had our life back.

There was one day that changed everything, though. I remember it was sunny. The morning began quietly. It felt like there was no war going on in the country. Around ten o'clock, I saw my dad through the window. He was outside, feeding the doves. He looked really calm. He looked different that day, I don't know why. A couple hours later, I was downstairs with our neighbor, pounding stale bread into pieces to feed to the doves. My mom had gone out to bake bread at a collective bakery. My older sister, Yelda, was cooking eggplant in the kitchen. My dad was going out to do errands with my younger sister, Maryam, who was three years old then. I was about eight myself. I heard Yelda ask my dad if he could go to the store to get some fresher eggplants. I heard her say goodbye to him and Maryam. I wanted to go with them, so I ran outside to try to catch them. But he was gone already, down the street. I followed him a minute, calling his name. When he heard, he turned around.

"Father, I want to go with you!" I said.

He said, "No. I can't take you. I can't take two kids. It's too dangerous." Then he told me to go home.

"Okay," I said. "But will you bring me some gum?"

I watched him walk down our narrow street, carrying my sister in his arms. Then I went back home.

When he left it was quiet, but soon, the bombs started exploding again. It would be quiet for ten minutes, and then more bombs. Some were close. Some were far away. I remember my neighbor yelling for us to get in the basement, where we would be safer. We went down there, and a bomb exploded very close by. Yelda was so startled, she dropped her paring knife. We were all shaking. A few minutes later, we heard a group of men's voices coming down our street.

They burst into our house. One of them was carrying my baby sister, Maryam, who was bleeding from her head. She'd been shot. They started washing her to see how badly she'd been wounded. She was so quiet, I knew it was serious. The women were all crying. I didn't even think about where my dad was. One of the guys asked me to take him to find my mother at the bakery. When she saw me walk in, she knew something was wrong. He told my mother to go home quickly. My mom started screaming and crying, dropping her things on the floor. When she got home, she found out that my sister had lived, but my dad had been killed. When she heard this, the day became night for her. She has never been the same again.

***

We were back at home when a group of men from the neighborhood opened the gate to our yard and carried my dad's body in on a stretcher. I was upstairs in the house, watching through the window. They laid him down inside the courtyard, close to where the doves' house was. He was covered with a white cloth. My mother called for me to come down and say goodbye, but at first I couldn't go. I had no strength in my legs. I felt like I couldn't move. Finally, I made it downstairs to see him. My mom lifted the cloth and put her hand up to close his eyes. We all hugged him and cried. Even the doves seemed to be crying, making sad sounds, banging their bodies against the wire of the cage as if they wanted to get out.

The road to the graveyard had been covered with landmines, so it was too dangerous to take him there. We decided it would be best to bury him next to the house in a small garden belonging to our family. On the day he was to be buried, he was laid on a stretcher in our backyard. My mom said, "I want the birds to say goodbye to him." She opened the cage and let them out. She was talking to him. She said, "These are your birds. I can't take care of them." She was angry—not at him, but at the war. Maryam, the two-year old, was still in the hospital. She would be brain-damaged for life. My mom said to my dad's body, "These birds remind me of you. I'm going to let them go away, like you have gone away."

As she opened the door, the doves flew out and, one by one, landed around the stretcher where my dad's body lay. They did not fly away. Some sat in the trees, watching. But they stayed close, sitting all around him. A mullah read from the Koran, and the men lifted the body to carry it to the garden. As they moved, the doves started to follow. They flew behind the men as they walked to the burial site—a long trail of doves following my father to his grave.

***

I was 14 years old when I moved to the United States with my mother and two of my sisters. My two older sisters are married. One lives in Kabul and the other in Canada. Life in Afghanistan was very hard for my mother, since she was responsible for taking care of our family all by herself. When the Taliban came to power, we lost all our freedoms. Women were not allowed to work anymore, and girls were not allowed to go to school. We were forced to go the mosque seven times a day to pray. If the Taliban caught people on the streets during prayer time, they would be arrested and taken away.

I am now a junior at Deering High School in Portland, Maine. My favorite class is English, because I learned it quickly. My two younger sisters go to school here, too, and my mother is learning English at Adult Education. I am thankful for my mom. If it were not for her, I would not live in the United States. I wouldn't have the opportunities for success that I have here. If I had stayed in my country, I would have been married at the age of 14. I'd probably have kids, and I wouldn't have a good life.

In my free time, I work at McDonald's, because I am

saving money to buy a car and to go to college. My life has changed a lot here. I am getting an education. I have a dream to become a dental hygienist and live in California one day, where it is warm. My hope is to become a citizen, so this land will be my land someday. And I'd like to be able to bring my older sister, Yelda, who lives in Kabul and is lonely there, here to Maine to be with us. More than anything, too, I want to grow up to be like my dad, because he was a kind person and everybody respected him for that. Even though I don't live there anymore, I care about Afghanistan, about the people there. I watch the news at night to see what is happening. It is never very optimistic. There is still war in my country, even with the U.S. helping there. There are still bombs exploding. People are still scared. My hope is for my country one day to become a peaceful land.

Ali Mohamed with story house model

Hyenas

Ali Mohamed

My grandmother always told me that I should be afraid of the lions, but not to be afraid of the hyenas. My grandmother lived in our village and helped my mother cook. She died before my father died, but I remember the stories that she told me. She said that you should never run away from a hyena because they will kill you, but if you don't run away, they will not kill you. My brothers and sisters were afraid of hyenas, but not me. They had seen a hyena eat something down by the river once, and it scared them.

At night, we put our goats inside the fence that went around the house. One morning, a hyena jumped the fence, grabbed a goat by its neck, and jumped back out of the fence. My father said to me, "Wake up! Go get that hyena who stole our goat!" So I ran after him. I hid behind a tree and when the hyena went by, I hit his kidneys with a club and he fell down. My grandmother had told me not to bother hitting them in the head. You can hit them all day in the head and nothing will happen, but if you hit them in the kidneys they will die, she said. My father ran over to me with a knife, and he gave the knife to me. He was afraid of the hyena. Then my father said, "Kill him!" I stabbed the knife into the hyena's stomach. That was the first time I killed a hyena. It was before my father died, and he died when I was five years old.

After that all the people in the village came to me and said, "Oh, you killed a hyena!" My grandmother had told me not to be afraid of hyenas and I wasn't afraid. When you are small like that, the big people think it is funny that you are not afraid, they think you are brave. My father was proud of me, too.

My father was a kind man and he was very tall, he was maybe ten or eleven feet tall! Well, I don't know how tall he was, I never asked him, "How tall are you, father?" But when we walked together, while going to the ocean or to town, and he held my hand I looked way up into the sky to see him. My mother says I am getting tall like my father.

There was a village in Somalia where I lived, when I was five, with my mother, father, my two brothers and my sister. There were maybe twenty-five farms in this village. We had a round house made of wood. Inside the house were two beds where we slept. There was one bed for my parents, one bed for my sister, and my brothers and me slept on the floor between them. Every day it took hours for my father to walk back and forth from the store he owned in a town nearby, where he sold food and soap and things like that. He would leave at six in the morning and he would return at six at night. Sometimes, my mother would send me to bring him his lunch, and I would walk there and back all by myself. Sometimes, I would return on a different road because I liked to go through the forest, but my parents told me not to go on that road because they thought I might get lost, or there might be animals in the forest. But I never got lost nor did I ever see any animals in the forest to be afraid of.

Nothing had ever happened in my village. It was a very quiet village. I don't think that anyone had ever been killed there before. It was a Sunday night. I remember everything about that night. It was in the summer of 1992. It was 12:30 a.m. We were all awake. There were men with big guns who surrounded our house. They looked like they were in the army. My mother said that we were the minority tribe, and they were fighting against us and that is why they were there. Or maybe they had seen my father coming from his store in the town and thought that my father had a lot of money.

One of them had a chopped off arm, there was no hand below his elbow. He seemed to be the commander and he was the worst of them. He told everyone to come out of the house and to lie down on the ground. He said, "Where is the father of this house?" My little three year-old-brother told them that my father was in the outhouse. Then the commander without a hand, without saying anything, shot him. Just like that, without thinking, he just shot him and he died. The soldiers went to the outhouse and kicked down the door. The outhouse was up on the rocks and there was no way he could have escaped from it. The commander with the chopped off arm told my father to come out, and when he did, the commander then told him to get on the ground. Nobody was moving. A few minutes later, the commander said to one of the soldiers, "Why are you looking at that man, kill him!" Then they shot my father. He died. My mother screamed, "Why did you kill him?" The soldiers asked the commander if they should shoot her. The commander didn't care about anything and he said, "Look at her!" and then he shot her. The shot hit her leg. She was alive, but badly injured.

They took everything we had. They took my father's store money, my mother's earrings, and anything good we had. Then they left, and people from the village came. A friend and my older brother, who was ten at the time, took my mother away in a cart pulled by a donkey to get her to someone who could help the wound in her leg. I tried to follow them but they told me to stay in the village. Some other villagers buried my father and my little brother.

When my brother got my mother to the doctor, they told him that there was nothing they could do for her. It was not a place where they could do surgery. My uncle gave someone some money so that she could go the hospital in Kenya. My uncle, my brother and my father's friend all took her there and she was in the hospital in Kenya for two or three years. I missed my mother for those long years. I lived with my sister in the village. She made cakes that we brought to the town to sell.

When my mother came back to Somalia to get me, my sister decided to move to another village, and we never saw her again. She got married and she has two children. My mother, my brother and I moved to the Hagadera, a refugee camp in Kenya. We lived there for two years. I liked it there. I had lots of friends, we played soccer, I went to school and learned English. I had a girlfriend there, she is still there and I still talk to her on the phone sometimes.

One time, my friends at the refugee camp and I were talking, and they said they didn't believe that I had killed a hyena. They were afraid of the hyenas. I told them to ask my mother if I had killed a hyena in my village. Then one morning, early, they took me over to the slaughter house where there were always hyenas lurking around. I told them to give me a club. I started running towards some hyenas, there were three or four together and then I dove on to the ground and grabbed the legs of one the hyenas, then I hit him in the kidneys, like my grandmother had told me to. That's how I killed that hyena. Then I took a rope and I tied his legs together. My friends said, "This is amazing that you can kill hyenas like that!" Then they said, "Every Friday we will come here and you will kill a hyena." But I said, "No."

I was fourteen when I killed that hyena and I lived in the refugee camp in Kenya. Now I am seventeen and I live on Merrill Street in Portland, Maine. It is peaceful here, except sometimes in my dreams. Coming to America has meant going back, again and again in my mind, to these stories I am telling. My mother wants me to forget, but I cannot. I would like someday to go back to Kenya, perhaps go to the university there. And I would like to ask my girlfriend there to marry me.

But I'm done killing hyenas. At least I hope so. I'm almost as tall as my father now, and I've nothing left to prove.

Aknowledgments:
the builders

In the spring of 2006, the groundwork for The Story House Project was laid in a series of pilot interviews with local immigrant high school students at the Salt Institute in downtown Portland. The Telling Room is deeply grateful to Donna Galluzzo and all the folks at the Salt Institute for giving the project a home base. Thanks also to Rebecca Stewart and Nancy Rosenbaum who were instrumental in helping to lift things up off the ground.

Phase one of the project began to take shape when Portland High Art teacher Allison Villani invited The Telling Room into her English as a Second Language Art Fundamentals class for a month-long series of creative writing workshops in the fall of 2006. Several of Allison's students became the backbone of the PHS group and her support has been crucial to the project's success at PHS. Other teachers and educators who helped launch Story House in their schools include Lori Stillman and Sue Stein at the Waynflete School, and Maureen Fox, Drew Pisani, Suzanne Dodson, and Sheri Oliva at Deering High School.

Many mentors, each a professional Maine writer, taped and transcribed lengthy interviews to arrive at stories spoken in the students' own words. Mentors worked with each storyteller to fine tune the narratives and polish each sentence. The long list of local poets and writers we want to thank for serving as mentors include Susan Conley, Sara Corbett, Lance Cromwell, Gibson Fay-LeBlanc, Rachel Graves, Patty Hagge, Ethan Howland, Molly McGrath, Allison Paige, Mike Paterniti, Lewis Robinson, and Kathy Sullivan. Other writers who helped along the way include Tyler Clements, Lily King, Mary McCann, Kent Pierce, and Peter Smith.

Thanks also to Dave Eggers and Valentino Achak Deng who came to Portland in February 2007 to discuss their collaboration on the novel, *What is the What: The Autobiography of Valentino Achak Deng*, as well as the social, political, and cultural situation of the Sudanese people, before an audience of over 500 people. Prior to the public event, Deng, a Sudanese "Lost Boy" who is now a student at Allegheny College, led a round-table discussion with Story House students and heard a few of their own coming to America stories. Portland High Senior Aruna Kenyi's response to this awe-inspiring meeting with Deng was to begin writing his own memoir—at last count, he was on page 160.

The second phase of Story House posed a challenge: translating the students' narratives into a three-dimensional exhibit to house the stories. Here the help of Maine College of Art Professor Christina Bechstein and MECA's Creative Community Partnership Coordinator Jennifer Christian was instrumental. In March, Bechstein's students began meeting with the high school storytellers to help them design and build a series of house-like sculptural structures using images and artwork from the stories. The first structure built by the MECA students and the storytellers was a temporary one: a homemade parachute they all sat under together to discuss their images of home. The MECA students helped each storyteller see how, collectively, they might all work together to create intimate, arresting spaces to honor the stories.

All of the people associated with the Maine College of Art's Art for Social Change course deserve profound thanks, including Professor Christina Bechstein, Jenna Crowder, Ashley Curry, Andy Dibella, Desiree Duell, Koko Evans, Erica Faughnan, Courtney Graf, Tori Marsh, Michelle Michaud, Kelly Noble, Pat O'Brien, Jona Rice, Liz Sofarelli-Deuben, Emily Staugaitis, Sydney Williams, Creative Community Partnership Coordinator Jennifer Christian, Erin Hutton in Student Affairs, photographer Sean Harris, Building Consultants David Siegfried and Michael Chestnut, Student Builder Dan Macleod, and Cross Cultural Consultant Jennifer Mancini from the Immigration & Refugee Center.

The Story House Project has really been a series of collaborations: teachers, students, working writers, local artists, art students, and many others who added expertise and support along the way. None of these collaborations would have been possible were it not for generous grants and contributions from the Davis Family Foundation, the Virginia Hodgkins Somers Foundation, Bread for the Journey, the Clements Family Foundation, and many community members. Blunt Youth Radio, the Salt Institute for Documentary Studies, MECA, the SPACE Gallery, USM, and WMPG provided integral support for this project. Ari Meil at Warren Machine, a local independent press, deserves particular thanks for helping us put this anthology together, as does photographer extraordinaire Laura Lewis, who has believed in the importance of documenting The Telling Room's work from the beginning. Poet and Telling Room Intern Heidi Thayer provided all manner of support, enthusiasm, and expertise during the entire process.

Lastly, thanks to each student storyteller. Your honesty, humor, and dedication to this project made it something everyone has been honored to participate in. You are the future of Portland.

Patty Hagge and Ridwan Hassan

About The Telling Room

The Telling Room is a group of local writers and teachers who believe children and young adults are natural storytellers. As Greater Portland's non-profit writing program for young writers between the ages of 8 and 18, we hope to meet each student's passion for stories with equal enthusiasm and provide role models for young writers. We hold writing workshops at the Salt Institute and in local schools; organize A Living Writers Series, which brings acclaimed writers to Maine to give public readings and work in small groups with student writers; publish anthologies of student work; and carry out special programs like The Story House project. Please check us out at www.tellingroom.org.